How To Conquer Your Fear Of Public Speaking

This Guide Will Show You How To Become A Confident Speaker By Following These Simple Steps!

By Sasha Diaz

Table of Contents

Introduction

Chapter 1: Why Public Speaking Matters

Chapter 2: The Fearful Fear

Chapter 3: Knock that Fear Down; Speak Yourself Up!

Conclusion

Introduction

I want to thank you and congratulate you for downloading the book, "How to Conquer Your Fear of Public Speaking".

This book contains proven steps and strategies on how you would be able to overcome your fear of speaking in front of your audience. Public speaking is an inevitable and essential activity in our lives. Regardless of where you live or where you go to work or school, you will always need to speak up in front of people. In this book, you will learn several ways on how you would be able to prepare yourself before you deliver your speech, enjoy the experience and give your best during the speech proper, and what to do once you have finally accomplished this task.

At the end of this book, I want you to be motivated to face your fear of speaking in public and realize that public speaking is not a difficult thing to do at all. I hope that you will be inspired to speak up.

Thanks again for downloading this book, I hope you enjoy it!

Go out there and ace that speech!

Chapter One

Why Public Speaking Matters

You might be wondering as of now why we have to speak in public. You might be asking: "Why do I even have to do public speeches when I know I have this fear of speaking in front of the people?"

So why does public speaking matter in the first place?

Public speaking is an essential part of our daily lives. The Saylor Foundation defined public speaking as the "process of designing a message to an audience." Effective public speaking is being able to understand your audience, speak goals to them, choose a topic for your speech that will involve your audience, and deliver the speech competently and in a way that will capture the attention and interest of your audience.

As a form of communication, public speaking is one of the best ways to convey a message to a large group of people. Even though most people don't notice the importance of public speaking, there will come a point in our lives when we will need it. Publicspeakingpower.com says that public speaking is a chance for each and every one of us to expand our leadership and influence among people, as well as to excel in our careers. Public speaking will also help us influence other people's thoughts and bring about positive change among others.

Moreover, public speaking is also a way to be able to share your own ideas and knowledge to other people. Always remember that an idea uncommunicated is like trash; no one will fully benefit from it. No matter how great your idea is, if you didn't communicate or share it with other people, it's useless.

Mastering the art of public speaking also helps you increase your level of confidence. How can you be confident when all you do is just sit in the corner and never stand up and speak for yourself? The only way you can boost your confidence when it comes to speaking in public is to do it yourself.

Public speaking will also make you more comfortable with other people, since they will be your audience. You will be able to speak to lots of people, even to strangers or those whom you barely know.

Public speaking also has relevance in your chosen career. If you are in business, public speaking will make you create a difference in your business. It will allow you to persuade more people if you can communicate to them effectively. If you are a student, on the other hand, public speaking will also be a part of your classes. Your teachers might ask you to share your ideas to your classmates so they can learn from you, or you can learn from their ideas.

Public speaking is an important part of our daily lives. It is inevitable, so if you have the fear of doing this, the only thing you can do is to knock that fear down and realize your fullest potential as a speaker. You never know, you might be the next most successful speaker out there.

Chapter Two

The Fearful Fear

Have you ever felt queasy whenever you have to stand in front of people? Have you ever had your hands and knees shake and your forehead produce a river of sweat every time you have to speak in public? Have you ever gone frozen in front of an audience, with your mouth starting to dry up and your heart beating as if there was no tomorrow? If so, then you might be suffering from the so-called Glossophobia, or the fear of public speaking.

Glossophobia is known to be one of the most common phobias around the globe. Statistically speaking, about 75% of Americans suffer from this fear to some degree. Because they feel anxious about being in front of the people—regardless of how many people there are—they just tend to avoid some events whenever they get the feeling that they'd be an object of everyone's attention in that gathering.

Warren Buffett, a billionaire investor, said that he was once terrified of speaking in public. He told Forbes Magazine that he was extremely nervous about having to speak in front of people, which is why he had to arrange his classes in college just to avoid those courses that require getting up in front of an audience.

"I lost my nerve," he spilled, referring to that public speaking course that he once took in college but eventually dropped out of before it even started.

Buffett is not the only one who has experienced such anxiety, because chances are you and the people around you are also experiencing this fear. Many famous personalities and leaders are also struggling or have struggled with the fear of public speaking.

Just like what has been mentioned earlier, public speaking is essential because it is a way to disseminate information and knowledge to other people, especially to a larger group of individuals. Since we live in an era wherein practically everyone is hungry for new information, it is important for knowledge to be well-communicated.

The problem, however, is that most of us are afraid of speaking in front of an audience, and even the mere thought of standing in front of a large group makes us nervous already.

Glossophobia.com, a site that talks about the cases of Glossophobia, listed down several symptoms of this speech anxiety. These symptoms include:

- intense anxiety or nervousness before verbally communicating with other people, or simply by thinking about having to do so;

- skipping events that focus the group's attention on each individual; and

- physical distress, nausea, or panic in any circumstance that involves public speaking.

But why do you—as well as the other people around you—have this fear of speaking in public?

It may be because you think that whatever you are going to say is unimportant or irrelevant to other people. You feel like once you started talking in front of them, they would just be yawning and couldn't care less about what you are talking about. It may also be because your parents would not allow you to speak for yourself as you grew up. You've always lived in their shadow so facing people makes you anxious. It may also be because you had a traumatic experience before wherein you were humiliated while you were speaking in public. Or you just let that feeling of anxiety in you to grow over time that you can no longer conquer your fear.

You might be feeling hopeless now, but you need not worry. Regardless of what caused you to feel anxious whenever you speak in public, there's still a way—or ways, rather—to overcome that fearful fear.

Chapter Three

Knock that fear down; speak yourself up!

You are now ready to speak yourself up, but you still feel quite anxious if you would be able to do it. Just remember these: prepare, relax, and do your best.

A. Before the speech

1. *Do your research*

You only feel nervous whenever you have to deliver a speech because you think you might fail, and the one and only reason why you would fail is because you didn't prepare. Before you can even come up with a good and decent speech, you have to be well-informed about your topic and you need to think about it thoroughly. The only way to do so is by researching.

Regardless of how difficult the topic for your speech is, you would feel confident about doing well once you have properly done your research. Researching unfolds the unknown. If you have been given a topic that you know nothing about, the first thing that you would do is scratch your head and say: "How am I going to talk about this when I am not even familiar with this subject?"

That is when your researching skills would come in. You can always make use of the internet and type on Google, Yahoo, or other search engines the topic that has been given to you. Before you even know it, you're already seeing a wall of information as well as resources that can help you learn more about your subject.

If you want to widen your knowledge about a particular matter, you have to read a lot for it is the only way to expand what you know about the topic. You have to know by your heart what you are going to talk about so that you will be able to come up with a speech that you can deliver smoothly.

2. *Practice, practice, and practice*

Nothing beats practice. As an old saying goes, "Practice makes perfect." This may sound cliché to many of us, but it still applies when it comes to performing well. Even Thomas Edison once said, "Genius is one percent inspiration, and 99 percent perspiration."

When you rehearse your speech, you can point out the mistakes that you make and then correct them. It is advisable that you do so in front of a mirror where you can see your entire body for you to be aware of the awkward gestures that you make while you speak. You can also exercise saying those words that you are having a hard time pronouncing so that you would no longer have a problem saying them when you're already delivering your speech. Trying some tongue twisters can also help you exercise your speaking skills. Start by saying each word slowly and repeat them while increasing speed. This will help you master how to speak properly at a suitable speed.

Read your speech repeatedly so that you can master every word, sentence, and any other part of it. Never, ever memorize your speech for it will not help you. Memorized things last shorter than those that you know really well, so do not even attempt to just memorize your speech. Rather, you have to know every part of it by heart, so that forgetting a word or a part of your speech will no longer be a problem.

Never take practicing for granted. Always keep in your mind that public speaking is unlike singing or dancing—it is not an inborn talent. Though there are people who happen to be born with the guts for public speaking, they still needed to practice a lot to improve their skills.

According to Forbes, the best way to deal with being nervous is practicing since what you do more often will become comfortable with you, thus making it less frightening. And since you've already practiced delivering your speech, there is no longer a reason for you to feel anxious about it because, hey, you've already done that before so you're fine.

3. *Throw the bad thoughts away*

We all know that what makes us feel worried about the thought of giving a speech is not really because we don't know what we do, but rather because we don't know what will happen at that exact moment once we're already on the stage and giving the speech.

You feel uneasy because you fear that you would be misjudged by the people that you will be giving your speech to. You're already creating the idea in your mind that while you're speaking in front, your audience is yawning and wondering if you could be any more boring. This mere thought will eventually discourage you and will bring you down, making you feel bad about yourself and think that you are not good enough.

Instead of thinking about the negatives, why don't you feed your mind with the positive mood? Smile in front of the mirror and tell yourself this: "I can do this. I can ace this speech." Say that for several times and you will find yourself feeling better and motivated to do your best.

4. *Relax*

Once you have already done your practice, the next thing you should do now is to relax. You should not exhaust yourself with too much practice; allow your brain to adjust to whatever information that it needs to retain.

Get a good night's sleep before your big day. You don't want your audience to doze off while you're speaking, so you too should not feel tired and sleepy during your speech proper. Have a good breakfast as well. Do not eat the foods that you are not comfortable eating. Do not drink coffee if you are not a coffee drinker (or if you are, then have some if it will help you feel relaxed). It is important to take good care of yourself for you to feel better.

When there are only a few minutes left before your speech, you should breathe properly and deeply from your diaphragm. Breathing is helpful for you to keep your composure as well as your voice. It also helps you feel relaxed.

To keep yourself from stumbling upon speaking, you may also perform a mouth exercise. Open your mouth as wide as you can, just like when you are yawning, while having your jaw move in circles and sideways. Do so for five times.

Another way for you to keep yourself from tensing is to try the technique called the wall push. This practice was done by the late actor Yul Brynner just before he did his performance. In this method, what you have to do is stand about one and a half feet away from a wall and just place your palm flatly on it while "pushing" the wall (hence the term wall push). While you do this, your abdominal muscles contract. As you exhale, hiss and contract your muscles just below your rib cage. Repeat this for a few times and it will help you knock all your anxiety and stage fright down.

One thing you can also do is talk to your friends about things other than your speech. This will help you relax even more and feel confident. And always keep in mind that since you have already practiced doing this, there is no longer a reason for you to be anxious about failing.

You can also think about your favorite speaker. Think about how he does his speeches all the time. What are the things that you like the most about him? Doing so will help you feel inspired to do your best, just like that person that you look up to.

B. During the speech

1. *Flash that smile*

Aside from the fact that smiling makes you look better and more confident, it also has an effect on your psychological well-being.

According to Psychology Today, smiling brings a positive mood to your brain. It activates the neural messaging that helps you feel better and brings a sense of happiness.

Smiling boosts the release of neuropeptide which helps you fight the feeling of being stressed. Since neuropeptides are molecules used by neurons to communicate with each other, they aid in sending messages all throughout the body when we're happy, sad, angry, depressed, stressed, and excited. Moreover, smiling also relaxes your body—it lowers your heart rate and blood pressure—thus helping you feel at ease when you are about to speak in public. It has also been said that smiling is contagious for it lifts the moods of the people around us.

Aside from its psychological effects, smiling also tells your audience that you are confident enough to stand right in front of them, thus making them give you their attention. No one would want to see a speaker biting his lip from time to time while speaking just because he's feeling nervous. No one would also want to see someone who frowns a lot. Always remember that it is a lot better to watch someone who uplifts people's moods and brings a positive attitude around.

2. *Stand straight*

Another article in Psychology Today showed that posture has a significant role in the way a person will behave in front of his or her colleagues. Once you're standing straight or at least having a proper posture, you develop the feeling that you have power and authority. "Posture is significant to a person's psychological manifestation or power than their title or rank alone," says Psychology Today.

If you are standing properly in front of the people as you speak, you create a sense of authority. You make yourself feel that you are in a higher position as compared to your audience. This will help boost your confidence since you will no longer feel intimidated by these people.

3. *Keep in mind that you don't look as nervous are you feel*

Once we have stepped on the stage or the podium, we feel like every eye is watching us. This feeling makes us anxious and insecure about what we are going to do. But you also have to remind yourself that your audience can't see you as being nervous as much as you feel. Thinking that people can see your hands and knees shake will not only make you feel queasier, but it will also block your mind from what you are going to say. You will be more focused on what people are thinking about you rather than on what you really are about to say.

Keep your mind away from thinking that you look uncomfortable in front of your audience. You have to focus on what you are really there for, rather than on how you are feeling.

4. *Think about your audience more than yourself*

Just like in point number 3, you have to stop thinking about how you look in front of people. You've had enough time preparing yourself before your speech, so you should be feeling confident about yourself by now.

Thinking too much about yourself will also make you feel conscious about it, thus causing you to lose your focus. Keep in mind your objective: to deliver your speech properly and have your audience learn from it. That's just it. At the end of the day, your audience will no longer even remember what you wore or what your hairstyle was (unless they took a photo with you because they found you amusing), but what will stay in their minds are the words that you said and how your speech has moved them.

5. *Do not depend on your notes*

While it can be helpful to bring notes on stage, you must never depend solely on reading your notes.

Notes only serve as your guide, just in case you are forgetting something. Resist the urge to look at your notes from time to time. Do not write every part of your speech on your note cards for it will only tempt you to just read your speech rather than really deliver it.

If you have prepared a PowerPoint presentation, refrain from looking at it every so often. Chances are you might lose track once you take a glance on your PowerPoint presentation. Remember that the only reason you prepared a PowerPoint presentation is for your audience to be able to understand what you are talking about, especially if your speech involves a lot of technical terms or if it requires diagrams and illustrations. It does not serve as your notes in delivering your speech.

Just keep this in mind: You are delivering a speech, and not reading a story.

6. *Movements won't hurt*

Do not be as stiff as a mannequin. Make use of hand gestures, especially if it will help you emphasize some points in your speech. If you are talking about something taller than you by a few inches, how would your audience visualize that if you wouldn't raise your hand a few inches above your head?

Movements will not only help you clear out some points, but it will also make you feel more comfortable standing in front of other people. If your hands keep on shaking, make sure you use some hand gestures as you speak so that your audience won't notice that your hands are trembling. Just don't use them too much, or else it will look annoying already. Also, if you can walk around the room, then make use of that opportunity as well. It will not only help you connect with your audience but it will also make you feel more confident as you deliver your speech.

7. *Connect with your audience*

One main rule in communication is to know your audience. After all, the communication process happens between you and your audience, so it is important to get to know them.

Do not look at your audience as if they are faceless walls. Think about how they feel while you are speaking. If they have confused looks on their faces, then probably they are missing some points of your speech. Do not talk fast as if you are running after something. Make every point clear to your audience. Always focus on the messages that you want to convey to them.

8. *Give it your best shot*

Just put it this way: your audience knows nothing about your topic and they are relying on the information that they will be getting from you. Though that is not totally the case, thinking about it this way will make you feel better about yourself and help you boost your confidence. Always keep in mind that you deserve to be heard. According to the Oral Communication program for Teaching and Learning in Stanford University, "The more you tailor your speech to your audience, the more they will listen and stay involved."

So do not stress yourself and just enjoy the experience.

C. After the speech

1. *Congratulate yourself*

You were able to finish something that is very hard for you such as giving a speech and you deserve a round of applause for that. Now, ask yourself: "How do I feel about this?" If you feel happy, then that only means you did very well.

Give yourself something that you really want as a reward for being able to get over your fear. By doing this, you will feel good about yourself and you will be motivated to continue and take the next step.

2. *Deal with the criticisms positively*

We all love taking compliments from others, but as much as we love receiving good comments, we must also take criticisms with a positive attitude. If someone said something bad about your speech, do not take it seriously, but instead consider it as a way to improve yourself in this field. Criticisms should not be meant to put you down, but rather to help you focus on the things that you need to develop.

3. *Face your fear*

There is no better way to conquer your fear than facing it. Public speaking is not something that happens only once and then just vanishes into thin air. It is something that should be done repeatedly, especially if you want to master the art of it. The more you do it, the more comfortable you'll feel about it.

Professional sports players don't just wake up one day with the strength and ability to play a game. The same thing goes with public speakers. It takes a lot of practice and effort before you can finally push that fear away. You can improve yourself by enrolling in public speaking courses. You can also spend time with the people who face the same fear as you do by joining a public speaking group. This will get you to meet people to support and encourage you to do better.

All you have to do is to know your fear and how to face it.

Conclusion

If you have fear of public speaking, do not let that fear take your success away from you. A lot of great opportunities can come to you once you know how to communicate to people very well.

Just because you are afraid to stand in front of people, it doesn't mean that you should avoid public speaking. That is never and will never be the answer. You are just tolerating your fear and you are not helping yourself to overcome it.

Stand up and speak out. Always remember that there is nothing wrong with committing mistakes, especially if this is your first time. Let go of the perfectionist in you and learn from your mistakes.

Keep in mind that nobody wants you to fail. Your audience is expecting a great performance from you so give them your best. You will eventually find them clapping their hands for you.

You deserve to be heard. Go ahead, get out of your shell and ace that speech!

Finally, if you enjoyed this book, please take the time to share your thoughts and post a review on Amazon. It'd be greatly appreciated!

Thank you and good luck!

www.ingramcontent.com/pod-product-compliance
Lightning Source LLC
Chambersburg PA
CBHW071602170526
45166CB00004B/1757